Doing Business in the UK

Klari-T

Copyright © 2017 KlariT
All rights reserved.
ISBN:1548909475
ISBN-13:9781548909475

1 UK CULTURE --------- 7
Moving Countries --------- 7
Mindset --------- 8
Characteristics of society --------- 8
Language --------- 9
Beliefs --------- 10
Lifestyle and aspirations --------- 10
Education --------- 11
History --------- 11
Geography --------- 11

2 ECONOMICS AND POLITICS --------- 12
Politics --------- 12
Economics --------- 13
Cost of living --------- 13
Fiscal year --------- 14
Attitudes to money --------- 14
Currency --------- 14

3 COMPANY TYPES --------- 15
Major industries --------- 16
Imports and exports --------- 17
Workforce --------- 18
Ethics --------- 18

Corporate citizenship and social responsibility ------------------ 18

Information sharing --- 19

Meeting people --- 19

Interpreters -- 20

Forms of address --- 20

4   BUSINESS ETIQUETTE ------------------------------- 22

Business cards --- 22

Body language --- 23

Communication styles -- 23

Customer service and suppliers ------------------------------------- 23

Working hours and holidays -- 24

Making appointments --- 25

5   TEAM WORK --- 26

Building trust -- 26

Team expectations --- 26

Time management --- 27

Dress code -- 28

Leadership styles --- 28

Delegation and supervision --- 29

Managing relationships --- 29

Coaching and mentoring --- 30

Recruitment -- 30

Feedback ---- 31

Motivating ---- 31

Managing conflict ---- 32

6 BUSINESS MEETINGS ---- 33

Planning ---- 33

During ---- 33

After a meeting ---- 34

Negotiating ---- 34

Decision making ---- 35

7 BUSINESS PRESENTATIONS ---- 37

Preparation ---- 37

Expectations ---- 37

8 BUSINESS ENTERTAINMENT ---- 39

Being a host ---- 39

Eating out ---- 40

Giving gifts ---- 40

9 USEFUL BUSINESS TERMS AND PHRASES --- 41

IDIOM MEANING ---- 41

10 . CULTURAL DIMENSIONS ---- 45

CULTURAL PROFILE ---- 45

Task versus relationship ---- 46

Direct versus Indirect -- 48

The Individual versus the collective --------------------------------- 50

Risk taking versus risk avoiding -------------------------------------- 52

Urgent versus relaxed -- 54

Power equality versus power distance ------------------------------ 56

Linear versus circular --- 58

Concrete versus abstract -- 60

Low context versus high context --- 62

11 FURTHER INFORMATION ------------------------ 64

Better Integration --- 64

1 UK Culture

Understanding cultural differences is one of the most important skills that organisations require in the 21st century. As business is becoming more global, the need for manager and teams to have a good understanding of cultural differences will enable them to work more effectively and innovatively. Whether you are working within your home culture within a culturally diverse team or working in a different culture, understanding the key values of different cultures will have a positive effect on you, your team and your organisation.

This book focuses on UK culture, and provides a good insight into the key values, expectations and social requirements for anyone wishing to live and work in the UK, work for a UK company or work within a team with British nationals.

Being British is about driving a German car to an Irish pub, grabbing an Indian curry or Turkish kebab on the way home, and sitting on Swedish furniture in front of a Japanese TV, watching American TV shows.

Moving Countries

Moving to another country or working with people from a different country is very difficult, but also one of the most requested skills in the 21st century.

The anxiety and stress of Culture shock is well recognised amongst those relocating, but is also becoming increasingly evident amongst those working within multi-cultural teams.

How you cope with culture shock will have a big impact on your future.

There are the obvious differences of language, location, weather, laws and food. But the real differences between social rules can be far reaching from finding childcare, getting your electric connected, or to knowing what to do in an emergency.

In a work environment, do you know what your boss will expect of you, how negotiations occur, the protocol for information sharing or how to give feedback.

This guide gives the basic information on the unique cultural elements within the country, to help you understand the key values of the nationals

Mindset

Mindset - is a set of assumptions or notions that are held by one or a group of people. it is so powerful that it is able to adapt and change behaviours. It is difficult to counteract the effect that mindset has on decision making and understanding.

- Reserved
- Heightened sense of fair play
- Nationalistic, island mentality
- Individual and private
- Pioneering, innovative and inventive
- Sceptical
- Tradition matters for the older generation
- Modernity is both reluctant and rapid.

Characteristics of society

Characteristics of Society - Societies need populations within which social relationships can be formed. To create these relationships, societies require: A sense of likeness, Differences to establish respect, Interdependence, Cooperation, Conflict, Change, Culture

- Individualistic and capitalist
- Inventive – over 50% of all inventions have been British
- Class structure
- Traditional
- Aging society but with little pension provision
- Highest divorce rate in Europe
- Melting pot of difference races
- High surveillance – large use of CCTV
- Crime is high. 1 in 10 people affected
- British debt is high.
- In the UK, people see themselves as British, English, Irish, Scottish or Welsh.
- They see themselves a slightly separated from Europe.
- They are not as patriotic as other countries except for sporting events.
- They are very proud of their heritage and of being pioneers throughout history.
- As well as being nationalistic towards their own section of the UK, regional pride can be seen within parts of Cornwall, northern and eastern England.
- Britain has a diverse society, with many general minorities gaining a strong voice.
- There are very large African, Caribbean, Indian, Jewish, Polish and Gurkha communities that continue to play a large part in British culture.
- Standards of living are high, but working hours are long.
- The UK is overcrowded and property prices are very high

Language

The main languages in the UK are:

    English

    Welsh (in wales)

    Scottish Gaelic (Scotland)

Welsh and Scottish TV produce programmes in their own languages

The British are not good at learning other languages as so many people speak English internationally.

- Implied, indirect and understated
- Informal
- Global language – has many variations
- Heavy use of jargon and acronyms
- Dialects – based on German, Latin, roman, Norman and Scandinavian

Beliefs

- Church and state never really united
- Church of England broke away from catholic church
- Church attendance low (under 4%)
- Catholics, church of England, Muslim, Hindu, Jewish, new age, and many others
- 72% population believe region is not important in today's society

Lifestyle and aspirations

Aspirations - are long term goals that motivate people. Motivation is very complex, but being part of a group improves motivation, and increases the changes of achieving your aspirations. The fear of being punished, gaining acceptance and approval from your peer group, and maintaining a certain level all impact group aspirations.

- Work to live – becoming more difficult
- Most Britons are stressed due to lack of time
- Little socializing with work colleagues
- High home ownership
- Materialistic and a throwaway society
- 50% of the population own 92% of the wealth
- Prefer to spend rather than save.

- More over 65s than any other generation.
- Most of the population have access to the internet

Education
- State comprehensive
- Public schools
- University – some subsidies
- Oxford and Cambridge
- Primary, middle and comprehensive levels
- Free education until 16 – occasionally to 19
- Universities are many and diverse

History
- Invasions – Roman, Nordic, Saxon, Viking, Angles
- Civil war – king and parliament
- Napoleonic wars
- American revolution
- Slave trade
- Industrial revolution
- Imperialism – British empire – own ¼ of the world
- WW1 WW2 Cold war
- EEC/EC/EU
- Thatcherism – first female prime minister years
- Britain rebranded – Blair
- Us market values versus European social values

Geography
- Island – separated from mainland Europe
- North – industrial / south – service
- London is capital but remote from country
- Population 63m
- Comprises – England, Scotland, wales and Northern Ireland
- Climate – mild, variable and wet
- Benefits from gulf stream.

2 ECONOMICS AND POLITICS

- Parliamentary democracy
- Low unemployment in 2016
- Energy sufficient
- Free market capitalism
- Industry is more private than public
- Labour/conservative / democrats / green / regional
- Conservative in power
- Prime minister – Theresa May – 2016
- Monarchy – queen Elizabeth since 1952
- Improving economy
- Common law

Politics

The UK has a democracy parliament with HM Queen Elizabeth II as head of state. Executive power is authorised to the government by HM The Queen. There are devolved governments within Scotland, Ireland and wales that also have this power.

There are two chambers within parliament - the house of commons where the members are elected and the house of lords. Other governmental parliaments can be found in the Scottish parliament and the Welsh and northern Irish assemblies. The highest court within the UK is the Supreme Court.

The UK has a multi-party system which currently included the conservative parliament, the labour parliament and the liberal democrats with many other smaller parties being involved at various points in history.

The constitution is made up of various factors which also currently includes EU law. This practice has also been adopted by other commonwealth or former commonwealth countries.

General elections are usually held over four years and it is the party that holds the most seats within the House of commons that take over leadership.

The Scottish National Party is currently very strong within Scotland, but recently voted again independence from the UK.

The biggest current issue within the UK is 'Brexit' In 2016 the UK voted to leave the EU and this is currently in progress. There is a lot of instability and uncertainty about this will proceed.

The Good Friday Agreement was signed to stop terrorism in Northern Ireland in 1998. The peace process is still ongoing

AS AT 2017:

PRIME MINISTER - THERESA MAY

CHANCELLOR - PHILIP HAMMOND

Economics

Since the Brexit decision (2016) the UK economy has begun to slowdown, and there are some concerns about the effect this slowdown will have on the country.

Prior to Brexit the economy was expected to slow a little but remain robust. The UK economy is still expected to grow faster than the Eurozone.

The UK is the sixth largest world economy; this was to drop after the Brexit decision was made, but is recovering.

Cost of living

- Living in the UK is 2.33% lower than living in the US
- A 3-course meal for two at a mid-range restaurant is £50
- Milk is £0.89
- Taxi (1 km) normal tariff £20.00
- 1 pair of jeans (Levi's or similar) £56.87

Fiscal year

The UK fiscal year runs from 1st April to 31 March for corporation tax and government financial statement purposes

Attitudes to money

- Many people within the UK save 'for a rainy day'.
- But they are also big spenders and borrowers
- Over 80 million credit and debit cards are in circulation
- The UK can be credited with two thirds of credit and debit cards transactions within Europe.
- Many Britons gamble - betting on horse racing, dog racing, casinos, gaming machines and the national lottery.

Currency

- The currency in use is the great British pound sterling
- Some companies, especially those near London, will trade in euros
- Notes are: £5, £10, £20 and £50
- Coins are: 1p, 2p, 5p, 10p, 20p, 50p, £1 and £2.
- Credit, debit and contactless cards are accepted in most places.
- Get up to date conversation rates from
  http://www.xe.com/

3 COMPANY TYPES

Most organisations within the UK are sole traders, partnerships, companies limited by liability or public limited companies that are listed on the stock exchange.

During the 1980s Margaret Thatcher and her government encouraged privatisation and sold many of the public companies that had previously been owned by the government - e.g. rail and mail services.

In the 1990s many companies began converting to the more efficient 'flattened organisation' process and began to focus on outsourcing.

Networking is important but loyalty is not taken into many business negotiations, meaning that most contracts are repeatedly out to tender.

There are a very high number of SME (small or medium enterprises) and entrepreneurs within the UK, which encourages the innovative and inventive spirit.

Government grants are provided to keep this sector buoyant, and lager organisation offer business space, meeting rooms and hot desking locations to encourage this work ethic.

Job sharing and flexi time is also encouraged to support working parents in all organisational types

Major industries

- Finance and banking
- Information technology
- Construction
- Oil and gas
- Government
- Healthcare
- Machine tools
- Manufacturing
- Electric power equipment
- Automation equipment
- Railroad equipment
- Shipbuilding
- Aircraft
- Clothing and other consumer goods
- Motor vehicles and parts
- Electronics and communications equipment
- Metals
- Chemicals
- Coal
- Petroleum
- Wholesale and retail
- Transportation
- Logistics
- Education
- Paper and paper products
- Food processing, textiles

Imports and exports

Imports

Almost $700 is imported

Aircraft and spacecraft
Finished manufactured goods
Machinery
Ships and boats
Clocks and watches
Pharmaceuticals
Fur and artificial fur
Live animals
Cereals and milk products
Railways and tram equipment
Musical instruments
Fuels
Food stuffs

Exports

Almost $500 billion is exported in goods.

The UK is the 9th largest exporter in the world.

Manufactured goods
Machines, engines, pumps
Gems and precious metals
Vehicles
Pharmaceuticals
Electronic equipment
Aircraft, spacecraft
Medical and technical equipment
Fuels
Organic Chemicals
Plastics
Food and beverages
Tobacco

They generally export to Germany, US, Netherlands, France, Ireland, Belgium

Workforce

- As of May 2016, 31.58m people work in Britain.
- 23.12m work full time
- 8.46m work part time
- 1.69m people unemployed
- 8.9m people of working age who don't work and are not looking for employment
- 26.69m employees
- 4.69 self-employed
- 28.15m UK nationals work
- 3.34 non-UK nationals work
- Average pay (excluding bonuses) is £468 per week.

Ethics

- Britain has a strong ethical code and bribes are very uncommon.
- Backhanders and commissions are provided for new business and are not always revealed.
- Many companies will however insist on transparency and keep 'gifts' very public.
- Cash bribes are not given but corporate entertaining is widely accepted.
- Tickets for big sporting events are often given.
- Civil servants are not allowed to take any hospitality offers.
- Some nepotism exists in family run companies, but in most places employees are judged on performance and results.
- Equal opportunity is important.

Corporate citizenship and social responsibility

- Corporate social responsibility is important in the UK.
- Companies of all sizes will be expected to have diverse policies and procedures on various environmental, economic and social policies.

- Job sharing, maternity and paternity packages, homeworking and flexitime are all important.
- British companies sponsor arts and cultural projects, they sponsor social activities and support less fortunate communities.
- Companies are expected to participate in voluntary schemes to develop world education and support the environment.

Information sharing

- Meetings are regularly held about information sharing.
- Communication channels are very open, but there is a real need to keep internal communications - internal.
- External information sharing is done via email, intranets, internets, newsletters, magazines, conferences, training sessions and marketing processes.
- The flat structure enables employees to ask questions of their superiors.
- Within external deals there is a lot of secrecy with use being made of 'non-disclosure agreements'.
- Bids and tenders can be sealed and held in secret.
- Pitching for business is often quite a closed affair.
- The public are protected by the Data Protection act which prevents companies from sharing, selling or exchanging their own personal information
- Business Etiquette

Meeting people

- British people can be contradictory by being open and friendly, but also being standoffish and reserved.
- Be yourself rather than trying to copy, as it is uniquely British.
- Don't be over enthusiastic at your first meeting, this will lead to them being suspicious.
- Do not boast or overestimate your own credentials.
- The British much prefer someone truthful, and accurate.
- Do not over apologise.
- Dress smartly but individuality is also accepted.

- Ironic or flamboyant ties can often be seen.

Interpreters

- Most business activities are discussed in English, even when being discussed internationally, as English is the global business language. Interpreters are available and will be used when required. The interpreters are very highly qualified.
- Larger conventions and events often have interpreters for foreign languages and also into sign language.
- Registered translation services and interpretation services are widely available throughout the UK.
- Legal documents and public records must be translated to English before being accepted by officials.
- Public services are often available in different languages. Multicultural support can often be found within the work place, and telephone interpretation services can be available.

Forms of address

- The handshake is the typical form of address.
- Men should wait for women to extend their hand, but this rarely occurs.
- A firm handshake is important especially for men, or they may be perceived as weak.
- Eye contact is important, and helps to cement relationships for future meetings.
- 'How do you do?' is a common greeting, but does not require any response.
- 'How are you?' is another greeting that only requires a response of 'I'm fine, thank you'.
- 'Pleased to meet you' also shows your views on meeting someone, and is commonly used, with eye contact and a smile.
- First names are used if known.
- More formally use Mr, Mrs or Miss along with their surname.

- The class system is very evident in first meetings, but is also very complicated so if unsure, use the formal approach.
- Initial meetings often include short conversations discussing the weather, traffic or travel to the meeting place.
- Humour is used within all elements of British contact. It can be self-deprecating or referring to current affairs or local issues.

4 BUSINESS ETIQUETTE

- The British are excellent at understatement and irony and this is used throughout the workplace.
- They also state the obvious whilst implying the opposite (sunny today, isn't it? when it's raining)
- Take note of tone of voice and facial expression - this will help understand the real meaning
- Learn to 'read between the lines'.
- Don't be offended - this is rarely the intention.
- Humour, jokes and anecdotes are a great way to build any relationship.
- Sarcasm is also used - 'nice weather for ducks' - very widely. This often shows unhappiness, disagreement or even contempt.
- Do not use the hard sell or put down the products of others.
- Even serious discussions will have light hearted moments.
- Excessive enthusiasm is discouraged, as much as excessive negativity.
- When in a business relationship, Britons can be blunt and very direct.
- The class system does impact British behaviour, but is rarely discussed. However, everyone is judged on their social skills and manners.
- Manners such as please, thank you, and sorry are very important.

Business cards

- Anyone can carry a business card.
- They are used for marketing as well as for providing a name remainder.
- Business cards are collected and stored for later use.
- Don't be offended if a business card goes straight into someone pocket.

Body language
- Public displays of affection are not common within British society, especially in the workplace.
- The younger generation are more affectionate than the older generation.
- The British are not tactile.
- Kissing, back slapping, elaborate handshaking is usually kept for friends and family.
- Personal space is important, don't stand too close - especially on public transport.
- Keep gestures to a minimum, however talking with your hands in your pockets is considered rude.
- Do not lose your cool. Keep your emotions in check.

Communication styles
- Management styles tend to be informed, focused, rational and pragmatic.
- They can also be indirect, unprecise and unwilling to state the obvious.
- Open ended questions are common.
- Communication can combine reality and experience.
- Managers are more subjective than objective about their role and their place within their organisation.
- Open verbal conflict is not encouraged.
- Keeping the peace within meetings and discussions is important. Avoid conflict.
- Implied language is common - we could consider..., could we look at other options, etc.
- Being told something is good, does not mean they like it. Check out tone of voice and facial expressions.
- Loud or overpowering speech is not tolerated in many environments.
- Manners, manners, manners.

Customer service and suppliers
- Britain has a strong service ethic and customer service is extremely important.

- It is widely used in corporate advertising as being a core business strength.
- It is a major factor in purchasing products throughout the country.
- British like to feel they are receiving a personal service.
- Call centres etc. are best placed within the UK, or within local, areas, as public backlash can be very strong and cause long lasting damage.
- Customer rights is widely discussed and promoted within the UK.
- There are television programmes, magazines and internet pages that discuss the benefits of good customer service and shame 'rogue traders'.
- Government watchdogs also monitor standards for water, telecommunications, education, energy and other areas of public service.
- Loyalty marketing is very big in the UK. Incentives are given to those who use products regularly in terms of cash back, discounts, loyalty clubs, special offers, points schemes and gifts.
- The corporate hospitality industry is also very large, with companies paying for company and team sporting events and galas.
- Companies moving into the UK, must consider customer service very carefully.
- Suppliers can be treated the opposite way, as customer ensure that products are price driven and value high.
- Small suppliers often have difficult credit terms to work with, continuous re-pitching

Working hours and holidays

- Working hours are generally 9am to 5pm, Monday to Friday
- However, most people work much longer hours
- Opening hours for shops are deregulated except on Sundays
- Sunday opening is typically from 10am to 4pm.
- Banks usually open from 9.30am to 4.30pm

- July and august are the school holidays in the UK
- Easter is a popular work break with many people going away to sunnier climates
- Bank holidays are at the beginning and end of May and also at the end of August.
- Most companies close or run on skeleton staff between Christmas and the new year
- The UK has fewer national holidays than any other European country.

Making appointments

- Make appointments in advance if possible, with confirmation if required.
- Do not cold call. This is not appreciated and is often met with hostility.
- Moving or re-arranging appointments is acceptable.
- Best appointment times tend to be mid-morning and mid afternoon
- Breakfast meetings are rare.
- Lunch and dinner meeting unusual.
- Appointments are often not denied or cancelled, but more avoided.
- Punctuality is quite important, but being a couple of minutes late will not cause offence.

5 TEAM WORK

- Team work is important within the British workplace.
- Being a good team player is a good quality, especially for a manager.
- Bad team players are viewed with suspicion or dislikes. They can also be seen as mavericks.
- Individualism is a positive attribute.
- Making decisions and taking responsibility is encouraged.
- Achievement and taking the initiative are also encouraged.
- Success should be kept low key, not flaunted

Building trust

- British people can be suspicious and difficult to assess.
- Trust is built by being open, honest and sincere
- Delivering results will increase our credibility
- Long term relationships are encouraged.
- The British are honourable and have a sense of fair play, so follow the expected procedures and rules to maintain trust.
- Do not go over someone's head
- Do not change plans without telling them
- Do not be deceptive.
- Britons are resistant to change, so handle changes with diplomacy and tact.
- Let people know what they can expect.
- Let people ask questions.
- Keep everyone informed

Team expectations

- There is an us and them culture in the UK.

- This has been there for many years and creates misunderstanding and miscommunication, poor productivity and reluctance to change.
- Teams are encouraged to self-manage, and be autonomous.
- Team members expect to be involved.
- Information should be freely available via emails, internet etc.
- Like some connections to immediate superiors and those higher up.
- Good team work should be promoted and celebrated
- Team building courses and training is common.
- Teams will socialise both in and outside work.
- Individuals will have their own targets as well has having team targets.
- Performance will be judged as an individual and a team.

Time management

- The longest working hours in Europe.
- Many people work between 65 to 80 hours a week, especially in the city.
- Lawyers and consultants will be expected to work through the night for an important deal.
- US companies working within the UK, expect their employees to be available for US hours.
- Emails and technology have exacerbated this with people being expected to reply throughout the night.
- Managers and employees are keen to be seen working and often spend more time at work than they should.
- This way of working is unhealthy and leads to stress and illness.
- Workloads and caseloads are high.
- Tight deadlines are common and are usually met.

- Public sector projects, however, rarely get completed on time or in budget.

Dress code
- There are a variety of dress codes within the UK.
- It is always advised to dress more formally for a first meeting if you have not been informed otherwise.
- Change to workplace dress code, asking questions if unsure.
- Business dress is a suit and tie for men with a skirt or trouser suit for women.
- Business casual is often shirt and trousers or skirt. Ironed and well presented.
- Dress down Friday - means that more informal clothing can be worn to work. In some places, this can include jeans and a t-shirt, but in other not. Check.
- Summer wear is also used by some companies to let employees be more comfortable in warmer weather.
- Dress does tend to be more formal in major cities like London.
- In general wear clothes that are appropriate, smart, and will not offend.

Leadership styles
- Leadership should be collaborative and consultative.
- Opinions and views should be actively sought after.
- Empowering staff is important in the UK.
- Collective ownership of positives and negatives is encouraged.
- Both personal accountability and collective responsibility is expected.
- A good leader is someone who remains calm. Under pressure.
- Leaders keep their emotions in check and remain confident throughout.
- Leaders should be approachable but not too close.
- They should remain objective when making difficult decisions that affect the team.

- British managers will challenge hierarchy and question motives and motivation.
- Challenge but show respect.
- 'Old school' leadership is still evident in some companies, where all the decisions are made by one person with a rigid structure. This is quite rare in corporate business.

Delegation and supervision

- British managers are good at delegating.
- Empowering the team is embedded in British culture.
- Teams work well together and delegated tasks get achieved as required and to deadlines.
- Teams take collective responsibility for delegated tasks and challenges.
- There is some caution in decision making as the fear of failure as a team is quite high.
- Meetings get held a lot to discuss the teamwork and processes of a delegated task.
- Company structure tend to be quite flat, so that superiors are easily accessible.

Managing relationships

- Measuring performance, benchmarking and relationship building is important.
- Suppliers are expected to hit the targets set, or the relationship will begin to fail.
- Managers and teams are also judged by their ability to meet targets and deadlines.
- Personal development, feedback, supervision, and coaching are all used to aid this process with workplace.
- Customer relationships are very important.
- Companies invest a great deal into customer retention and service.
- British customers expect good service and good results.
- They can become aggressive and litigious if they feel let down by a company.
- All companies are warned of getting customer service right.

Coaching and mentoring

- Coaching and mentoring are recognised ways of improving employee performance
- It is thought that about 90% of business use these techniques.
- Personal coaching can be provided by both internal and external coaches, traditional or peer to peer buddies or mentoring.
- Senior and middle management can often be provided one to one coaching
- Board members also have the option of coaches to improve key interpersonal skills such as communication and co-operation.
- Graduate entrepreneurial mentoring schemes are common.
- Mentors can support through the first few months or through particularly difficult areas.
- Mentors can provide support for many years.

Recruitment

- At senior level recruitment is often done via head hunters who are looking for a person with specific competences and skills.
- Employment agencies, newspapers, and internet advertising are all good sources for recruitment. · Graduate job fairs travel around universities.
- Big incentives are offered to those with the right skill base.
- Job advertisements cannot discriminate by age, sex, religion, race, disability or sexual orientation.
- These elements cannot be discussed within an interview.
- Interviews are carried out via a panel or on a one to one basis.
- Interviews can be long and include various tasks to show skill sets.
- Interviewees are expected to provide references, a CV and qualifications.

- More than one interview can be had and for higher levels salary is not discussed at the initial stages.
- There is a flexible job market in the UK
- The unemployment level is usually less than 5%.
- Professional and well-paid jobs need a high level of English language
- If you are studying and looking for work to cover daily costs, this can generally be done in pubs, bars and shops.
- Job types can vary from fulltime, part time, contractor, freelance, temporary and voluntary.
- Currently (pre-Brexit) EU nationals can work freely in the UK
- Non-EU nationals require a work permit – gov.uk

Feedback

- Feedback is an expected part of business in the UK.
- Employees expect regular feedback that is given on a one to one basis with their superior.
- Targets are set and challenged regularly.
- Individuals can work towards personal, team and company goals.
- One to one evaluation is also a time allocated for the employee to give superior feedback as well.

Motivating

- Accountability is far higher within the UK than across Europe.
- Britain is obsessed with measuring, and will measure itself against anything and everything.
- Companies produce lists and targets and aims that are distributed to motivate and enthuse.
- Individual performance management identified competencies around which individual behaviour can be benchmarked.
- · 360-degree feedback, coaching, mentoring, appraisal interviews, assessment centres and online development programmes are all designed to inspire and encourage individual improvement.

- British human resources departments are considered to be heading the training and development processes within Europe.
- Motivating others is important in creating an accepting attitude towards change.

Managing conflict

- There are many tribunals through the UK.
- Managing conflict is therefore an important element within company culture.
- Tribunals are expensive, badly publicised and time consuming.
- The department for trade and industry uses the employment act to encourage employees and employers to resolve workplace disputes.
- All employees need a three-point disciplinary and grievance process.
- This should include a letter, a face to face meeting and appeal meeting if necessary.
- If this procedure is not used the employee tribunal has the power to alter compensation payments.
- Bullying and harassment are the major causes of conflict and much money is spent providing training to prevent this.
- Discrimination is not widely found due to enforced legislation.
- Dignity and respect is expected behaviour in all work places.
- Middle and senior managers are encouraged to resolve bullying cases.
- Most companies will offer support and training in conflict resolution.

"ALONE WE CAN DO SO LITTLE, TOGETHER WE CAN DO SO MUCH."

--HELEN KELLER

6 BUSINESS MEETINGS

- Meetings are held for information sharing, discussion and decision making.
- Meetings are productive.
- Meetings are frequent due to the collaborative and inclusive way of working in Britain.
- Most people would prefer fewer meetings.
- Little time is spent preparing for meeting, but this is counterproductive.
- Being able to 'wing it' with little preparation is seen as a good trait but thorough preparation is always advisable.
- Meetings usually have an agenda

Planning

- Notify attendees in writing
- Give information on where and when the meeting will take place.
- Make sure rooms, equipment and speakers are booked beforehand.
- Video conferencing is common and equipment should be tested if possible before use.
- Conference calling by phone is often used and can be seen as quick

During

- **The chair usually runs the meeting, and may be a manager.**
- **Someone usually takes the minutes in a formal meeting, as a record of the discussions and outcomes.**
- **The agenda is followed, and can include deviations, interruptions and discussions.**
- **People may leave the meeting to take calls etc.**

After a meeting

- Minutes are circulated to those that attended and requested minutes
- If there are no minutes, an email is usually sent to anyone with a task to complete.

Negotiating

- Negotiations are influenced by the industry rather than by UK attitudes
- A neutral environment is encouraged for discussions to take place.
- Structure is important and is shared before the process
- Schedules and agendas are followed - no surprises accepted.
- Negotiating can be done between two individuals or groups
- Lawyers can be present, especially for bigger deals
- Bargaining is not common in the UK, but some counter offering will take place
- Start from a point near to your finishing point.
- Starting from a high point will mean you are not taken seriously.
- Commercial benefit is important in negotiating. · Negotiations are concluded by signed, binding contracts.

Decision making

- Decision making is done by consensus
- Input from those both above and below the decision maker's status will be consulted if necessary.
- Decision making can be influenced heavily by the short term financial markets.
- Managers must exceed targets and as such make fast decisions.
- Target setting is found everywhere within the UK
- Quick wins are used to demonstrate progress
- To influence a decision your understanding of the quick win is important.
- Always build consensus
- Highlighting pitfalls and risks will be respected
- Optimism will be viewed as naïve or suspicious.
- The hard sell will not be tolerated.
- Do not put people in a position where they have to make a decision.
- Decision process can be slow and laborious. Don't push.

7 BUSINESS PRESENTATIONS

British presenters often come across as confident with a natural ability to get ideas across to their audiences, this may be due to them having more confidence in speaking English.

Presenter training is common, and good courses can be expensive. · CEO's are given support to cover events such as Shareholder and Annual General Meetings (AGMs).

Preparation
- Do not try to give a hard sell or hype.
- Make sure the presentation has a focus.
- Extremes of behaviour are discouraged - excessive praise or negative feedback
- Doodling or staring out the window are common, but people are also listening to everything.
- Use media and technology to enhance not explain.
- Long term relationships are encouraged.
- Quick results are also encouraged.
- Sales pitches must show immediate benefits
- Back up information with analysis and figures
- Include some humour to keep audiences awake and interested, except when the audience is vocally unhappy.
- Always include a summary slide with notes to take away if appropriate

Expectations
- Audiences have short attention spans
- Give idea of time the presentation will take and the expected outcomes.
- Allow some time for questions
- A large audience will voice its pleasure or displeasure
- Allow time for a reaction after giving information, especially for a large group.

- When asked a question, listen and then respond.
- Do not appear insincere

8 BUSINESS ENTERTAINMENT

- If an 'entertaining' meeting is to be held then it is usually lunch.
- Working lunches rarely include alcohol and include work.
- An after-work drink or supper can be arranged to catch up on team ideas, gossip but not for serious discussions.
- Dinner is usually for a special celebration -such as someone leaving, being promoted etc.
- Lunch is usually between 12noon and 2pm.
- Dinner can be served between 7am and 11pm.
- Cafes, pubs etc. will serve work appropriate food or snacks all day.

Being a host

- Drinking alcohol is limited during the work day due to drink driving laws, inefficient working afternoons and alcohol bans on business premises.
- Drinking socially after work is more acceptable.
- You may be invited to the pub after work, because you are part of the team, rather than being a friend.
- If you wish to invite people - invite those at the same professional level as yourself.
- Hosting a formal event - get everyone's dietary requirements especially if you have a fixed menu.
- Always include a vegetarian option.
- Organise a private room if needed.
- The formal host will pay for dinner and/or drinks beforehand.
- Wine and menus can be chosen in advance.
- Networking before the sit-down meals starts is acceptable.
- Use a seating plan if desired.

- The host is usually sated at the head of the table or at the centre.
- Hosts often provide a small gift especially if it is corporate entertainment.

Eating out

- Relationships are created and nurtured after work.
- There is little distinction between work and private life.
- Lunch could be a pub meal or 'sarnie' (sandwich), but also be a full three course meal.
- Breakfast meetings can be held for those who travel long distances and stay in hotels etc. - business travel.
- Business meals are relaxed and issues outside of the workplace can be discussed.
- Table manners are important.
- Don't speak with your mouth full, don't reach across the table and don't make gestures whilst holding cutlery.

Giving gifts

- In a business environment (clients, suppliers etc.) this is heavily discouraged between individuals to prevent ethical issues.
- Civil servants are not allowed to accept gifts under any circumstances.
- Corporate hospitality is widespread throughout business to groups or whole companies.
- Entertainment hospitality is a large UK business.
- With groups being invited to sporting events, charity evenings, galas etc.
- Workplaces often have processes for dealing with special events such as birthdays, weddings, etc.

9 USEFUL BUSINESS TERMS AND PHRASES

The UK uses a lot of jargon and technical language. In order to keep this simple and understandable, the Plain English Campaign aims to keep public documents published in plain English.

IDIOM MEANING

24/7	Means 24 hours a day, 7 days a week - always open
A tough break	When something unfortunate or unexpected happens to disrupt plans
Agenda	A list of discussion points often for a meeting
Ahead of the pack	This means to be better or more advanced than others - usually your competition
ASAP	An acronym for 'as soon as possible'
At stake	Something at risk, potentially of being lost
At loggerheads	In dispute over something
At the 11th hour	At the last minute
Back to square one	To start something all over again
back to the drawing board	To return to the planning stage and start again
ballpark number/figure	A rough, guessed estimate
behind someone's back	To do something without informing someone and often unkind or unfair
behind the scenes	What happens in secret or away from view
big picture	Everything that is involved with a particular situation is called "the big picture."
blue collar	A blue collar works with their hands and can be an engineer, a manufacturer etc
Bring something to the table	Make an offer when negotiating
by the book	To do things by following the rules
call it a day	Finish something often for good

catch someone off guard	Surprise someone by doing something unexpected
change of pace	To do something different to your usual routine
cut corners	To do something cheaply - Often substandard construction or materials
cut one's losses	To stop doing something before you lose more money, knowing that you have already lost the money and time invested
cut-throat	Intense and aggressive - usually referring to sales
fifty-fifty	Divided equally - 50%
Flag up	Draw attention to Flapping Panicking or worrying unnecessarily
game plan	strategy
get back in/into the swing of things	To re-start something after having a break
get down to business	Stop talking about things in general and begin talking about the reason we are meeting
get something off the ground	To start something
get/be on the good side of someone	To do something that will make someone happy or like you
give someone a pat on the back	To tell someone they did a good job
Need it yesterday	Needed immediately/urgently
nine-to-five	A normal job, with a typical day lasting 8 hours
no brainer	An easy decision to make
no strings attached	When something is given or offered with no expectation to repay or return the favour
no time to lose	Time is short and the task must be completed quickly
off the top of one's head	To respond or comment on something without thinking it through. Usually an initial immediate response to something
On a shoestring	With very limited finances/funds
on the ball	To be aware of things involved with a project or topic
on the same page	Agreement about something

on top of something	In control and acting towards an outcome
on your toes	Be alert and cautious
out in the open	Public knowledge
Over the moon	Thrilled, happy, excited
put all one's eggs in one basket	Means that success is reliant upon one thing
Quid	£1
raise the bar	Set standards or expectations higher
read between the lines	Not just listen to the words, but take into account the situation, location, body language and context
red tape	rules
rock the boat	Cause a problem or upset a situation
round-the-clock	24 hours a day
run/go around in circles	To do the same thing over and over again, Often without a successful result
same boat	In the same situation
second nature	Something a person usually does automatically without thinking too much
see eye to eye	In agreement
see something through	Keep working at something until it is finished
sever ties	End relationship or break a contract
shoot something down	Reject a proposal or idea
sky's the limit	Anything and everything can be achieved
small talk	Conversational chit chat. Discussing the weather or what you did at the weekend
start off on the right foot	Begin something positively
start off on the wrong foot	Begin something negatively
state of the art	Modern and technologically advanced
take something lying down	Accept something unpleasant or unwanted without arguing back
take the bull by the horns	Confront someone directly

talk someone into something	Convince someone to do something
talk someone out of something	Convince someone not to do something
the elephant in the room	An obvious problem or situation that no one wants to talk about
The city	London's financial centre
The smoke	London
think big	Be ambitious and have big goals
think outside the box	Be creative, unconventional and innovative
throw in the towel	To quit, stop or leave
twist someone's arm	Persuade someone to do something that they don't want to do
Two-way street	Neither side benefits, information can be passed and received
under the table	Do something secretly
up in the air	Something has been left undecided
uphill battle	Achieving something that is very difficult and has many obstacles or barriers
upper hand	You have the advantage
white collar	A white-collar worker is someone who works in an office
win-win situation	Everyone gains something
word of mouth	Spreading information through conversation

10. CULTURAL DIMENSIONS

CULTURAL PROFILE

The cultural profile graph gives a visual indication of potential differences between cultures. By including another culture to the graph, you would be able to identify and be aware of major differences and also similarities. Understanding the differences means that you can change your communication style to avoid conflict.

This graph shows the typical profile of a British national, and although everyone is uniquely different, comparing typical profiles gives you an awareness of the differences you could encounter, and enables you to be better prepared.

For example, a Chinese national moving to Britain will have to change from thinking about the team first, to thinking about themselves first.

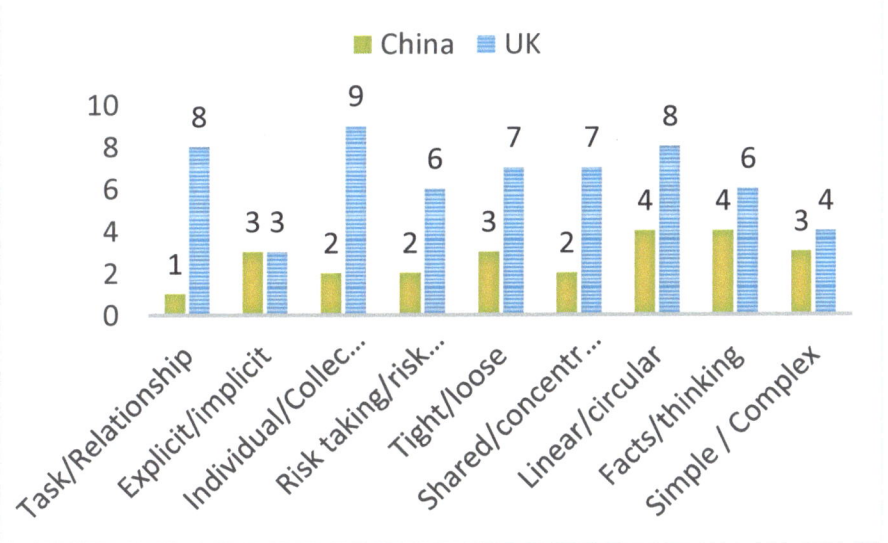

Task versus relationship

TASK	RELATIONSHIP
Impersonal. Let's get down to business.	Can I trust you? Are you loyal? Things get done when the right relationships are in place
Rules before relationship.	
Things get done when the right plans and processes are in place.	"I am spending time with Fred today. Maybe go to the museum"
"I have an appointment to visit the museum with Fred. I must be there by 2pm.	Maintaining relationships, good judgement, social skills and loyalty leads to success.
Accomplishments, and responsibility leads to success.	Decisions made by the group – can be wide ranging
Decisions made by individuals. Often a quick process	

- UK is task focused
- Business does not require a relationship – but is preferred if time and circumstance allowed.
- The British are competitive
- Success is based on objectives and hard targets
- Modesty should be maintained
- A strong focus on team spirit
- Fair play and failure are taught from a young age.
- British old boy network still exists but they are losing their power to results and experiences.
- They work long hours
- The UK is results driven.
- Focus on bottom line and performance
- Management processes are popular – Benchmarking, Prince, Six sigma s etc

- Follow the rules although may are unwritten and/or unspoken.
- There is an expected behavioural code.
- Independence is important.

This can affect
- Sales and marketing
- Recruitment
- Contracts
- Building trust

Direct versus Indirect

DIRECT

Say what you mean. Mean what you say

Literal truthfulness is valued within a business environment.

Often linked to task based cultures.

Saying 'no' or 'I don't know' is viewed as honest.

Business conversations rarely taken personally.

INDIRECT

Meaning often has to be taken from body language and inference, as well as words.

Direct communication is seen as impolite or rude.

Often linked to relationship based cultures.

Yes, is often used to show willingness or politeness, even if it cannot be achieved.

Any conversation can lead to embarrassment.

- The UK is implicit and indirect
- Language is ambiguous and humorous
- Feelings and intentions can be hidden
- Avoid confrontation and argument
- Tone down extremes of negativity or positivity
- The British will understate everything
- Emotions are seen as unprofessional.
- Physical contact is usually a handshake, and very close friends and colleagues may hug or back slap.
- Humour is a very big part of British life and is usually difficult to understand.
- Humour is used to break silences, diffuse situations, criticise and build rapport.
- Insider jokes specific to groups, teams or companies build groups and team working.
- Written communication tends to be formal, but this is changing with the advent of emails etc.

- Formal greetings and endings remain in emails.
- Some reports are written in everyday English but there are many still written in formal, professional legal speak.

This can affect
- Negotiating
- Coaching and supporting
- Conflict management
- Information sharing

The Individual versus the collective

INDIVIDUAL	COLLECTIVE
Me before we.	We before me.
Less consideration of the past and the present. The future is important.	Tradition and customs are very important.
Competition	Collaboration.
Individual achievement is important.	The success of the group is very important.
Study and hard work are rewarded.	Position is given.
Spending on assets is encouraged to show success.	Spending in the form of gifts and celebrations is important.

- Individualism is important – 'I' before 'we'
- The younger generation (millennials) are encouraged to express themselves, their talents and put themselves first
- The UK is a migrant population with young people leaving home at a young age, and families rarely living close together.
- Moving to another town or country is common
- Many people choose not to have children, to focus and develop a career and lifestyle.
- Finance is not a deterrent to raising a family.
- Fairness and equality is important
- Each person's voice, opinion and objections should be heard, regardless of status
- Loyalty to the company is not common, unless there is another affiliation such as religion, community etc
- Teamwork is appreciated and valued, but accountability is individual.
- Targets can be both team and individual

This can affect
- Teamwork
- Motivation
- Feedback
- Decision making

Risk taking versus risk avoiding

RISK TAKING	RISK AVOIDING
Make change happen; act decisively. New is good.	Avoid change. Steady, but sure. Stress continuity.
High tolerance for uncertainty.	Low tolerance to uncertainty.
Higher levels of innovation and change.	Loyalty is encouraged.
Flexible attitude to deadlines (usually shorter).	Traditional gender roles
More informal or spontaneous activities and projects.	Projects, processes etc. are well planned.
May be many different elements to a project at one time.	Rules, regulation and legislation

- Tradition is important within British culture
- The past is preserved and acknowledged through traditions held throughout the year, such as poppy day in November
- There is a strong sense of pageantry and ritual especially within the monarchy, the government and the law
- There is a strong island mentality
- The strength of Britain has meant that there has been little change for many years.
- The British have been victorious in wars and battles and this has led to a strong sense of identity.
- In reality, there is little substance to the British identity
- Resistance to foreign influences is strong
- Simultaneously acceptance of foreign influences is also strong.
- A live and let live attitude

- Keen to separate further from Europe, preferring to be British than European.
- A lot of control within the UK. It is the most watched country in the world (CCTV etc)
- New technology is welcomed specially to reduce crime
- New capital is not often found for new ventures such as prisons, schools etc
- New capital for industry and ideas can be found within a large range of funding options, but generally from private investors, not banks.
- Learning from best practice is preferred to void risk when possible
- The British are very unforgiving of failure, and you can be renowned for failure, more than success.
- They will keep up with technology, competition, innovation etc but can be reluctant in this.

This can affect
- Controlling
- Investing
- Managing change
- Planning

Urgent versus relaxed

URGENT	RELAXED
Be Punctual, control time. Time is money.	Be Flexible, go with the flow. Things will happen in their own time.
Complete one section before moving on to the next.	Information, sections and decisions can be revisited and repeated many times.
Rapport/relationship building is not important, unless it can be done quickly.	Time should be taken to build a good rapport, to allow a relationship to develop.
Tight timescales and deadlines are key to good business	Timescales are rarely issued and more rarely achieved.

- They aim to be punctual at all times, although this may not be possible, although people are forgiving if the effort has been made to arrive on time,
- Deadlines are important and generally met, but they are not obsessed with these.
- A deadline is often seen as a promise, and that you are morally obliged to deliver. Your business can be damaged if this is consistently broken.
- Stress is common in the UK, often due to the lack of time, and tight schedules.
- Being busy is seen as a good virtue.
- Retailing has incredibly long hours with availability being the key to success. 24-hour shopping is now common in the UK.
- Business is fast, with hard targets and short-term vision.
- Email is the most common form of communication due to its speed, and all businesses have a website.

- Websites are used to encourage 24-hour information, research or shopping.
- For meetings and presentations time keeping is more important if of a higher level, or multi-disciplinary. It is good practice to recognise the value of others time.
- Project and team meetings are often more flexible, due to the pressures of 'work'
- Social bonding and conversation is acceptable in many business meetings at the beginning or end.

Areas of impact
- Scheduling
- Meeting deadlines
- Project management
- appointments

Power equality versus power distance

POWER EQUALITY	POWER DISTANCE
Distribute power and authority within the group – collective.	Focus power and authority on specific people in the group – centralised.
A belief that everyone should have the same opportunity to succeed.	A belief that your personal distance from power is a fact of life that rarely changes
You often know the person who makes decisions.	Subordinates are dependent on decision makers.
Subordinates and decision makers are interdependent.	People are not equal and everyone has their place.
People are ready and expected to approach and/or contradict their superiors.	The powerful have privileges.
Everyone has privileges	

- The British respect hierarchy and birth right, e.g. the monarchy.
- It has a class society, but people are not prevented from moving between the classes.
- Accent, appearance and possessions can indicate a person's class.
- Historic powers such as the monarchy, the House of Lords, and the Old Boy club are losing their power, and are subject to reform.
- More women are in business, and hold senior positions.
- Regional accents are found across all TV networks, with the traditional RP (queens accent) being rarely used.

- Businesses often use a flat structure, giving power to more people, and giving everyone the opportunity to comment and advance.
- Recruitment is based on professional qualifications, and experience, not who you know.
- Managers are respected but re not expected to 'know everything'. They are expected to give credit to any specialists in their teams.
- Delegation is important.
- Empowerment and inclusion keeps employees engaged and dedicated
- Individual are expected to make their own judgements and decisions.
- Fairness and justice is important in British business.
- Respect ethnicity, ability, religion, sex, etc
- Diversity policies are built into company culture

This can affect
- Organising
- Leading
- Delegating
- Decision making

Linear versus circular

LINEAR	CIRCULAR
Analytical step by step process toward solution.	Focus on exploring and integrating perspectives in a relatively unstructured way.
Western culture.	
Lines divide – man/nature, subject/object, mind/matter	Eastern/Chinese culture.
	Circles enclose – interdependence, relativity and integration.
Individuality – goals, perspectives, interest, achievements.	Integrity – community, harmony, group objectives, safeguarding.
Future – the past has happened and the present is uncontrollable.	Tradition – the past loops and repeats, therefore it should be respected and learnt from.

- The British prefer step by step planning and performance
- Performance measurements are found within every aspect of organisations
- Efficiency and results are key motivators.
- There are a huge range of individual management products to help measure and monitor performance
- Companies measure their own performance in areas such as customer service, finance, logistics, strategy etc
- The government also use performance management systems for schools (OFSTED), medical, crime and legal services.
- League tables are produced to show the best performing schools, hospitals, doctors surgeries etc.
- Most elements are linear – in meetings an agenda is issued and then followed throughout the meeting

- In a meeting, the chairperson is responsible for the flow and adhesion to the agenda.
- At the end of a meeting the minutes are usually issued.
- Quick decisions and solutions are preferred
- Too much discussion is seen as unnecessary.
- Good relationships are encouraged but are not required.

This can affect
- Standardisation
- Problem solving
- Implementation
- Meetings
- management

Concrete versus abstract

CONCRETE	ABSTRACT
Emphasis on data and concrete experiences.	Emphasis on reasoning, concepts and logic.
Does not often reflect or consider areas outside of process or procedure.	Reflect on events, attributes, relationships and potential outcomes.
Projects are carried out one at a time.	Uses different scenarios to create different environments.
Change is not expected after the process has begun.	Planning and running multiple projects is usual.
	Outcome can be different to the plan. Change is expected.

- the British are pragmatic, practical, positive and sensible
- they are more likely to work things out during the process rather than by analysis beforehand.
- They aim for completion not perfection.
- Can complete a task with little preparation, but often to a good standard
- 'thinking on your feet; is a good quality
- They put down too much thinking and analysis, and see it of less value, preferring to learn from doing. – Learn from your mistakes.
- Doctoral titles are reserved for academics.
- Many business leaders are 'self-made'.
- PowerPoint is common and used for simplicity, clarity and speed. Bullet points are common.
- Decision making will focus on finances, data and hard, proven facts.

- Simple solutions are preferred to complex time consuming ones

This can affect
- Data gathering
- Evaluation
- Problem analysis
- persuading

Low context versus high context

LOW	HIGH
Reduce to basics. Focus on essentials with little context.	Focus on developing a detailed, contextual understanding.
Societal connections are shorter and there are many.	Societal connections have been developed over very many years.
Expected behaviours do have to be explained.	Explicit cultural behaviour is not needed, as everyone knows.
Wider networks with defined roles and tasks.	Complicated, multi-topic networks based on relationships.
Cultural knowledge is spoken of.	Cultural Knowledge is known.
simple	complex

- Explanations can be complex, due to contributing factors but processes are likely to be simplified
- Brief, concise, simple explanations are preferred. – get straight to the point.
- Fairness. Politeness and consideration of others is expected.
- Being pushy is considered rude.
- Consensus of all those involved is preferred where possible
- Communication is implicit so information is delivered indirectly, which can lead to confusion for some.
- The British will avoid conflict where possible, and may deflect and avoid the issue to prevent this happening.
- Tackling issues directly can also be seen as rude.

- Use bullet points during presentations and written forms, but never in direct speech.
- Politeness in speaking, and salutations is important.

This can affect
- Knowledge transfer
- Report and memo writing
- Presentations
- Making proposals

11 FURTHER INFORMATION

This guide was produced by Klari-T. Klari-T are specialists in Business English and Relocation.

Our advisers are specialists within the Business English field and also include an MBA Consultant. The focus on adapting to culture and communication emerged when many of our English learners encountered difficulty in adapting to new cultures despite speaking the local language.

By understanding the key values of the country you are living and working in, you are able to understand and adapt to some of the differences that you will experience. This will make you a much better communicator and feel that you are able to integrate with your new environment, rather than live on the edge or leave the country completely.

If you would like more materials please visit:

>www.chatterboxenglish.com

Or contact us on:

>Hello@chatterboxenglish.com

Better Integration

In order to integrate as quickly and painlessly as possible, it is best to compare your own personal culture with your chosen country.

If you would like to get an extra country profile, please email hello@chatterboxenglish.com .

www.ingramcontent.com/pod-product-compliance
Lightning Source LLC
Chambersburg PA
CBHW041106180526
45172CB00001B/129